SCENES *of America*

BRIDGEPORT

SCENES

of America

BRIDGEPORT

MARY K. WITKOWSKI

AND BRUCE WILLIAMS

ISBN 0-7385-4639-9

Published by Arcadia Publishing
Charleston SC, Chicago IL, Portsmouth NH, San Francisco CA

Library of Congress control number: 2006927567

For all general information contact Arcadia Publishing at:
Telephone 843-853-2070
Fax 843-853-0044
E-mail sales@arcadiapublishing.com
For customer service and orders:
Toll-Free 1-888-313-2665

Visit us on the Internet at www.arcadiapublishing.com

On the cover: The oyster dredges *Mollie M*, *Ellen S*, and *Fearless* are seen here tied up in Bridgeport Harbor around 1910. These dredges were typical of the steam- or gasoline-powered vessels built at the beginning of the 20th century to work on private beds in the sound. The *Fearless* was built in Maine as a schooner and later converted to power. (From the John Kochiss collection.)

CONTENTS

SODERHOLM'S
Butter-Krust
BREAD
IN BRIDGEPORT"

INTRODUCTION

Bridgeport, a New England coastal city, often does not know it is a coastal city. Emphasis is placed on Interstate 95, speeding in and out of the city, to and from New York, or on Route 8, heading north to the suburbs.

Yet Bridgeport is indeed a New England coastal city, with a history as such. Glimmers of this history can be found in the Historical Collections Department at the Bridgeport Public Library, back in shelves in the library stacks. Old volumes labeled "U.S. Customs House, License of Vessels," dated as early as 1797, show ship after ship going out of Bridgeport, carrying cargo from exotic places like the West Indies, captained by local names such as Capt. John Brooks or Captain Burroughs.

Our Bridgeport ancestors used Long Island Sound for their livelihood. They used it for fishing and for transporting goods. Many residents chose (and still choose) to live near the water; residents such as P. T. Barnum placed his house facing the sound, so the fine Long Island shore breezes helped soothe the heat of inland life.

On every corner of Bridgeport, in a faded sign on the side of a building, on an aging storefront, or in the rows of factory buildings still lining pockets of the city, there are clues to the workers of Bridgeport's past.

A good detective could put these clues together to solve the mystery. Collecting and deciphering the photographs of the last two centuries, one could figure out the thing that bound all the former Bridgeport citizens together: working together. Whether it was doing a job in a factory, raising a flag, helping to sell war bonds in World War I, developing public housing, or building a float for a parade, everyone was working together for the common good. Photographer Brewer H. Sholund took the 1919 aerial view of Seaside Park, seen on page 2, from a biplane. Carl Soderholm poses with his Model T Ford around 1912 in the photograph on page 6. Soderholm's bakery in the city's west end was especially known for its Swedish rye bread.

Most of the people in these photographs are not alive today. We can, however, look at the clues that they have left behind to see how their spirit and their work drove them through the obstacles of war, depression, and financial instability.

They say there is nothing new under the sun. Knowing that, revisiting these scenes of Bridgeport's best and worst times, we can all pause to reflect on these photographs and feel cheered that cities regenerate through the work of those who live there.

Mary K. Witkowski
Bridgeport City Historian

ONE

THE EARLY DAYS

This 1824 hand-drawn map shows details of the Bridgeport Harbor area. Numerous wharves line Water Street, and drawings of ships highlight the captains that sailed out of the harbor to the West Indies and exotic ports of call. Fayerweather, Burroughs, Hawley, and DeForest are some of the names of early shipping merchants.

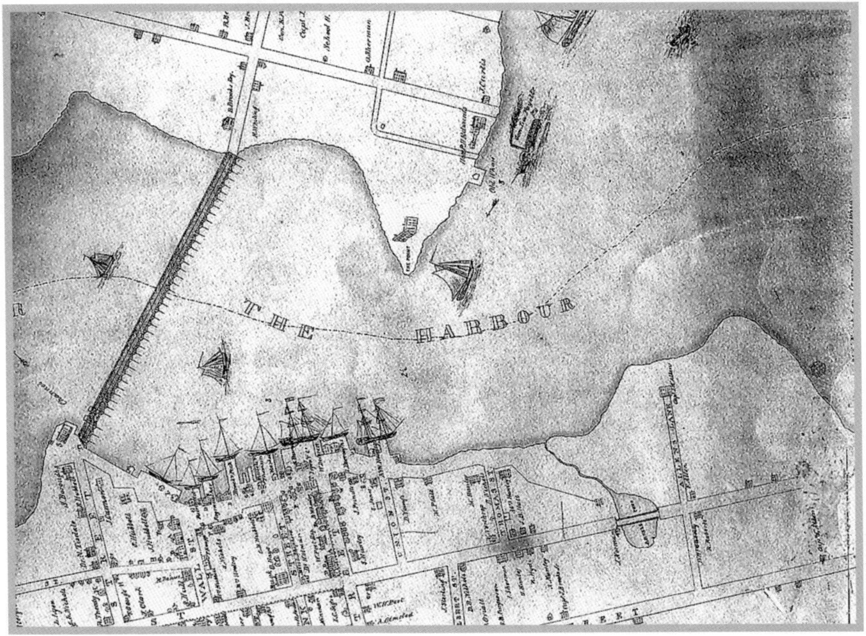
THE HARBOUR

The earliest known photograph of Bridgeport is actually of a building being remodeled. The Bridgeport Bank (founded in 1806) was the first bank to obtain a charter in Fairfield County. This photograph of the building at Main and Bank Streets was taken in 1856.

P. T. Barnum—museum curator, circus showman, and the city's most famous resident—worked to attract friends and colleagues to settle in his hometown. Although Barnum's scheme to bring the Jerome Clock Company to the East Side failed and ruined Barnum financially, industrialists Elias Howe and Nathaniel Wheeler eventually located their factories in East Bridgeport. Here Barnum stands with one of his successful endeavors, Commodore Nutt.

OPPOSITE: Washington Park was born when P. T. Barnum and Gen. William Noble acted as early city planners and developers, selling land near the Pequonnock River as the New Pasture Lots. Envisioning an area of industrial development and worker housing, they named the streets after their own families. Helen Street was named after one of Barnum's daughters; and, of course, Noble and Barnum Avenues are still busy thoroughfares in Bridgeport's East Side. Shown is a segment of the 1857 map of Bridgeport.

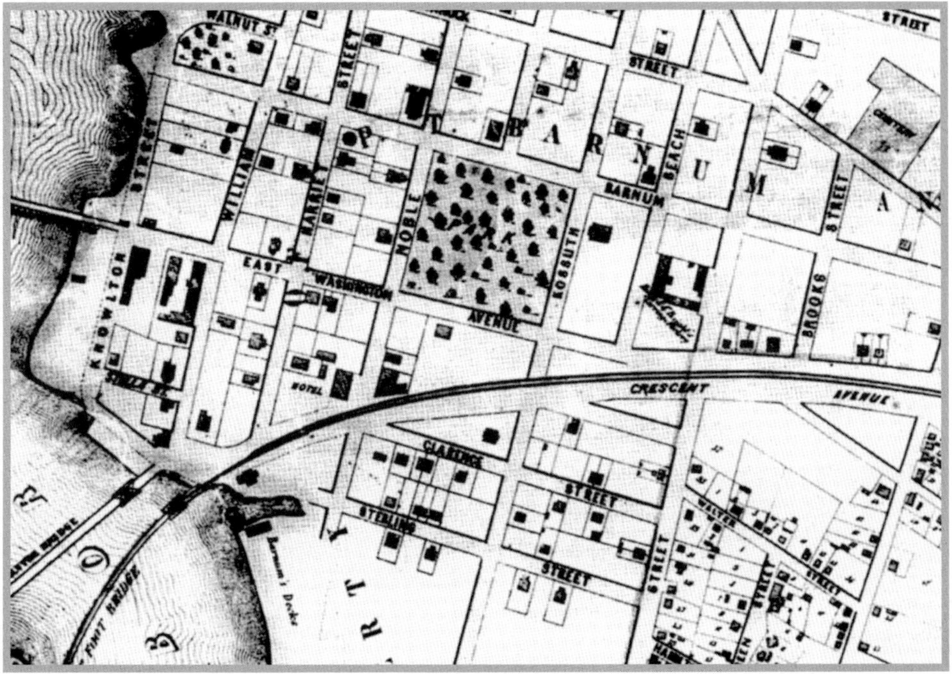
WALNUT ST.
STREET
WILLIAM
NOBLE
PARK
BARNUM
BEACH
KOSSUTH
BROOKS
EAST WASHINGTON AVENUE
KNOWLTON
HOTEL
CRESCENT AVENUE
CLARENCE
STERLING
WALTER
Barnum's Docks

In October 1876, employees of the Warner Brothers factory gathered outside of the Atlantic and Lafayette Street building to have a photograph taken. While a few male employees are shown on the right, the company employed many females as seamstresses. Many of the women were very young and, as in this photograph, some were girls. Before child labor laws of the 20th century, children often worked in factories.

Pictured in front of his Frisbie pie wagon in 1880 is Charles Fagan.

FRISBIE
KOSSUTH

D.H. STERLING

Even before Bridgeport became a city, a fire department of some sort existed. A bucket brigade, a volunteer effort of pulling water from the nearby Pequonnock River, was first used as early as 1796. Citizens had to own their own leather buckets and helped others put out fires. This firehouse on John Street near Courtland Street was named for Daniel H. Sterling, Bridgeport's mayor from 1860 to 1862. This c. 1880 photograph shows the horse-drawn steamer, a thing of beauty—horses and steamer shined to perfection by hardworking firemen.

Owning a funeral parlor was a new business in late-19th-century Bridgeport. Local undertaker Louis Abriola recalled a huge funeral procession led by a band playing dirges, followed by 30 horse-drawn carriages, and finally the funeral director driving a hearse. Not all funerals were that elaborate, but just as today, every ethnic group had its customs. Here John Cullinan and Frederick C. Mullins, who normally buried people of Irish heritage, smile for the camera around 1880.

R. T. WHITING.
THE BURROUGHS PUBLIC LIBRARY BUILDING

R. T. Whiting, Grocer was located in the Burroughs Building at the corner of John and Main Streets. Beginning in 1881, the original Bridgeport Public Library was located in this building. A sign for the library can be seen to the right of the men.

Since the 1800s, the city has had a police department, originally relying on volunteers to patrol the streets. The first chief of police was designated in 1869 and, by 1885, when this photograph was taken, the Bridgeport City Police Department was a full-fledged city department. According to the 1885 annual report for the police department, the most numerous cases were 153 charges of theft, 578 acts of drunkenness, 13 cases of fraud, and 110 cases of breach of peace. Police had reported other crimes such as Sunday ball playing, one case of carrying a deadly weapon, and two cases of killing ducks. One of the many duties of the police officers was the job of extinguishing gaslights in the streets.

In 1888, the Bridgeport Grain Elevator (left) towers over the harbor in the western view across the Bridgeport Harbor. Several vessels lie along the Water Street side, including a lighter, oyster steamer and the steamer *Rosedale* (far upper right) at its pier just south of the Stratford Avenue Bridge. In the foreground a gentleman sculls a sharpie, a type of vessel developed in New Haven for both oystering and pleasure use.

P. T. Barnum lived in Waldemere with his family for 20 years, enjoying the house that became cluttered with many treasures from his travels. Charity Barnum died in November 1873, when P. T. was traveling in Europe. While in England, P. T. secretly married a young English woman, Nancy Fish, on February 14, 1874. He returned to the United States after the marriage, keeping his marriage to Fish a secret. In September 1874, P. T. married her in a civil marriage in New York, bringing her home to Waldemere to live. In 1888, he began building a new home for his young bride, a less drafty home with electric lighting and good plumbing. The new brick house was built right next to the old house. The house was named Marina, once again showing Barnum's love of the sea. When Waldemere was dismantled, part of it was moved to 624 Atlantic Street and the other to 1 Pauline Street in Lordship, where they are still located.

DAVID TRUBEE & CO.

Shown here is a view looking north on Water Street around 1890. The David Trubee and Company warehouses can be seen on the lower left. Beyond the Stratford Avenue Bridge are the Wheeler and Howes Coal Company and the Frank Miller Lumber Yard. Currently, the Water Street area is the site of the new passenger terminal for the Bridgeport and Port Jefferson Steamboat Company ferries. The terminal also serves as the headquarters for the Bridgeport Port Authority and Harbormaster's Department.

Shown here is an 1890s view from the Stratford Avenue Bridge. To the left is the dock of the Old Mohawk Yacht Club, once located on the south side of the bridge. In the center of the photograph is the oyster boat anchorage known as the "pen."

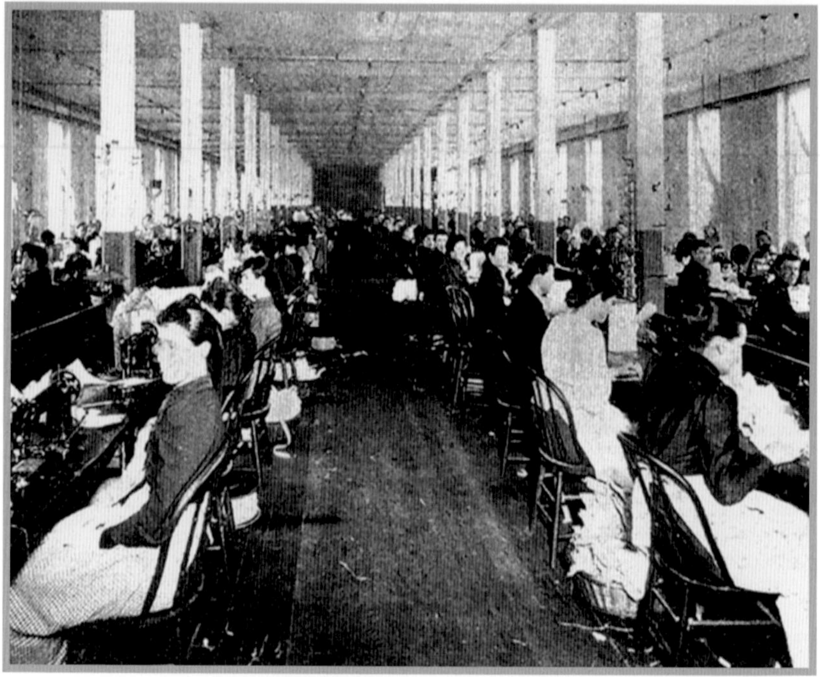

Women workers sew in the Warner Factory around 1890. Note the uncomfortable wooden chairs in which the women had to sit for long hours.

Bridgeport Hospital, completed in 1884 on Grant Street, was one of the most modern hospital buildings in the country. Designed by architects Lambert and Bunnell, the hospital was a pet project of P. T. Barnum, who became the president of the first board of directors of the hospital. The board of directors named Catherine Pettengill, Susan Hubbell, and Frances Elizabeth Pomeroy as founders of the hospital, due to the large endowment the women had contributed to the establishment. The final cost of the construction of the hospital was $120,508. Shown is the east ward of the hospital around 1890.

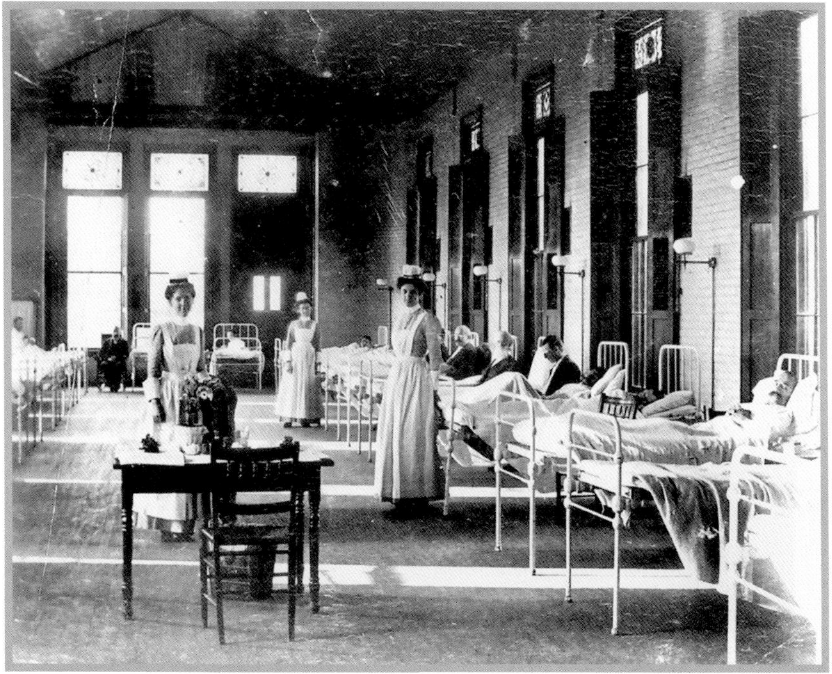

Originally a club for people interested in horses, the Seaside Club changed its focus with the dawn of the automobile age—it became a social club. The club started in 1884, meeting in some rooms of Main Street. In 1891, this building on Lafayette Street became the Seaside Club's permanent home. When the club moved out, the *Bridgeport Times-Star* newspaper used this building for offices.

In 1892, a huge celebration took place to honor Columbus's landing in America. Hundreds of residents lined the shores of Seaside Park to witness a ceremony that had A. H. Davis assuming the role of Christopher Columbus, while the harbormaster, Capt. John McNeil, stretched his arm out in greeting, carefully negotiating a plank on the rocky shores of Long Island Sound.

The vessels *Meta*, *Anita*, and *Stella* wrecked near the Shore House of the old George Hotel (now the Black Rock Yacht Club building) after a July 1893 hurricane. In an interview with the *New York World* magazine in 1889, lighthouse keeper Kate Moore related, "Sometimes there were more than two hundred sailing vessels in here at night, and some nights there were as many as three or four wrecks so you may judge how essential it was that they see our light."

Electric trolley cars were first used in Bridgeport in 1894 and, by 1906, trolley lines ran throughout the city. Trolleys could take people to their favorite destination, be it Newfield Park to play baseball, or Seaside Park to take a swim, as this Main Street trolley's signs showed. In the winter, problems arose when the tracks became covered with drifts, making it difficult for trolleys to continue their routes. When cars and buses became a more familiar mode of transit, many of the trolley lines were shut down. The East Main Street and North Main Street trolleys were the last to run in Bridgeport, taking their final trip in 1937. Removal of trolley tracks began with the state coordinating efforts between the city and Works Progress Administration workers in the 1930s.

NEWFIELD GROUNDS
TO DAY
MAIN ST.
AND
SEASIDE PARK
SHOW
BRIDGEPORT
JUNE
13

The old powerhouse channel cuts through the Cilco terminal property on Seaview Avenue. In the late 19th century, its banks were lined with squatters' cabins, shown here around 1895.

TWO

A NEW CENTURY

Yearly, a multipaged booklet would be printed showing the current year's activities for Pleasure Beach. In 1897, this booklet showed the various highlights at the park: the best bicycle track in all of New England, fine swimming, baseball games, and the annual baby contest.

OPPOSITE: This photograph of the inside of Pleasure Beach was taken by Lew Corbit in 1939. On the right are the arcades, while the roller coaster is in the background.

ICE CREAM PARLOR
FUN

Imagine waking up one morning and seeing a herd of elephants outside the front door. In Bridgeport's West End in the years 1881 to 1927, it was no dream. The Barnum and Bailey elephant trainers and circus workers corral the animals in the muddy field at the corner of Norman and Cottage Streets in the 1920s. Living in the area were circus performers, including Mabel Stark, who trained lion cubs in her basement.

Pedestrians walking near the railroad station prior to 1902 had to walk quickly to dodge the incoming trains as they came into the station. Train tracks were level with the street, so elevating the tracks became a matter of safety for local residents. Many a politician, including P. T. Barnum himself, campaigned to elevate the train tracks.

Tow lines from tugs operated by the Merritt, Chapman, and Scott Company attempt to pull the schooner *Perry Setzer* off damaged ways at the Greene Brothers shipyard on Seaview Avenue. Although being stuck on the ways at launching was considered a bad omen for a vessel, the *Setzer* had a relatively long career. Primarily engaged in the coaling trade, it worked steadily until lost on a shoal off North Carolina in 1924.

Fayerweather Lighthouse was built at the end of Fayerweather Island in 1823, replacing an earlier light knocked down during a great storm in 1821. Until 1851, when the first lighthouse was constructed off Bridgeport Harbor, it was the only beacon from Stratford Point to Norwalk. The light was in operation until 1933, when the U.S. Lighthouse Service discontinued its operation. In this 1905 view, the light's small oil house is seen to the right. The oil house, which held a supply of sperm whale oil for the light's eight lamps, was destroyed by vandals in the 1960s. In 1998, the light was completely restored with funding provided by the Black Rock Community Council and the City of Bridgeport.

"The most modern and the most complete automobile plant in this country" is how advertisements described the Locomobile plant at the beginning of the 20th century. The company was founded in Newton, Massachusetts, in 1899, but soon after moved to Bridgeport at the foot of Main Street near Seaside Park. Here is a 1907 look at the inside of the factory.

The Anchorage, shown around 1909, was built by financier Percy Bartram in 1904. The estate sits near the entrance to Black Rock Harbor on the site of the old Squire's Wharf. According to legend, the pirate Captain Kidd was thought to have buried treasure on the sandy shore near the house. To this day, the shoreline surrounding the house is known as "Money Beach."

The Bridgeport and Port Jefferson Steamboat Company has operated a cross-sound ferry service without interruption since 1883. Its first vessel, the *Nonwantuc*, was replaced by the durable *Park City*, built in Port Jefferson in 1898. The firm added a second vessel, the *Long Island*, in 1924. The *Park City*, shown here embarking passengers at Port Jefferson around 1910, was altered in 1921 to transport automobiles as well as walk-on traffic. A new *Park City* now sails the cross-sound route along with the *Grand Republic* (1968) and the *P. T. Barnum*, launched in 1999.

PARK CITY
PARK CITY

Seaside Park was planned out carefully by the foremost landscape architects of the day: Frederick Law Olmsted and Calvert Vaux, designers of Central Park in New York. It was P. T. Barnum who inspired other residents—such as Capt. John Brooks, Capt. Burr Knapp, and Gen. William Noble—to give land to make a marine rural park, the first of its kind in the United States. This photograph was taken around 1910 by T. S. Bronson. (Courtesy of the New Haven Colony Historical Society.)

Taken in May 1915, this photograph shows the building site of what one year later was among the busiest plants in Bridgeport's history—the Remington Arms and Union Metallic Company. The factory was built in a matter of months: in January 1915, the construction contract was given out; in March, ground was broken; and by November 21, enormous buildings had been completed.

ARMS - U.M.C. CO
BRIDGEPORT, CONN.
JAMES STEWART & CO., INC.

QUESTIONS
LEVERS

A roofer by trade, Socialist Jasper McLevy served as mayor for 24 years, from 1933 to 1957. Mayor McLevy lead Bridgeport through the critical years of the Depression, World War II, and the postwar years. Here Mayor McLevy pulls the lever and votes.

Bridgeport had the first dental hygiene school in the world, started by Dr. Alfred Fones, an 1890 graduate of the New York College of Dentistry. His father, Civilion Fones, also a dentist, served as mayor of Bridgeport from 1886 to 1887. Alfred Fones became a crusader in early oral hygiene and education. He opened his office at 10 Washington Avenue in a carriage house and, in 1913, opened a dental hygiene school on the premises. Thirty-four women were accepted into the first class at the Fones dental hygiene school. Many of them were mature women, schoolteachers, nurses, and doctors' wives. Dr. Fones and his assistant Irene Newman taught classes, inviting instructors from nearby Yale to speak. This c. 1915 photograph of the early classroom shows the young women practicing on Boy Scouts.

The Locomobile became a symbol of luxury in the American psyche. Producing only four cars a day in the plant, the company used the best materials: silver accessories by Tiffany, velvet and silk upholstery, and electric intercoms. Presidents and royalty purchased the car all over the world. Using extravagant advertising, the ornate advertisements featured every detail of the vehicles. Often photographs were taken of Locomobiles using the beauty of Seaside Park to emphasize the car's elegance and extravagance. This town model was designed and built for Elsie French Vanderbilt in 1916, it is shown here in Seaside Park.

Orlo Lindsley advertised that families could have their clothes laundered "on short notice" and "where theatrical troupes and traveling men can get accommodated." The laundry was only a half-block from the train station. Pembroke Laundry is still in business today, on Madison Avenue in Bridgeport. The Minty family has owned Pembroke Laundry since 1917. Shown is a horse-drawn laundry truck near the old city hall, now McLevy Hall.

The
PEMBROKE LAUNDRY.
BERGER CONNOR—BERGER

CONN.

The 1917 building on the corner of State and Main Streets was designed by Cass Gilbert for the Bridgeport Savings Bank, which later merged into what is now People's Bank. The building was built with Vermont Imperial Danby marble and limestone. Bridgeport Savings Bank and People's Bank merged in 1926 to become Bridgeport People's Savings Bank. The 1917 bank structure is now home to Roberto's, a popular Italian restaurant. In this photograph, workers are busy completing the inside details of the structure.

THREE

CHALLENGE AND CHANGE

Women's roles changed drastically during World War I. At Ellison's Auto Tire and Repair Company, seen here in this c. 1918 photograph, a woman works as a mechanic fixing an engine as a man looks on. Notice the Ford sign in the window of the business, which was located at 371 Fairfield Avenue.

Franklin Delano Roosevelt visited the naval base in Black Rock during World War I. Navy secretary at the time, he was escorted by Mayor Clifford Wilson and other Bridgeport dignitaries. He also visited the Lake Torpedo Boat Company; the Remington Arms Plant, which had just been completed in 1915; and other factories.

MOTOR CAR CO.
Pullman

In this horse-drawn float are women in costume, with a sign that reads United War Work. On Park Avenue, an unidentified black photographer stands in the forefront with a camera, ready to take a picture. Taken in 1918, this photograph also shows people gathered on the steps of decorator E. B. Ellis's house.

This cannon arrived by train in 1900, having last been used in the Battle of Santiago in the Spanish-American War. When it was first placed in the southeast corner forming Point Lookout, two piles of cannon balls were placed near the cannon. The cannon balls have since disappeared. Often people sit on the cannon for a photograph, as these women did around 1920. This photograph is from the Charles Callahan estate.

LEHIGH COAL
SOUTHERN NEW ENGLAND
ICE
No45
CO.

The Southern New England Ice Company would cut ice on Bunnell's pond in Beardsley Park during the winter and peddle it from house to house in a horse-drawn wagon. In 1929, more than 60,000 tons of ice were harvested from the Beardsley Park pond and were then stored in the icehouse. Eventually, the Southern New England Ice Company began manufacturing ice in a Knowlton Street plant, where it still manufactures tons of ice per day.

The Bridgeport Lighthouse, shown here around 1930, marked the entrance to Bridgeport Harbor. The federal government constructed the lighthouse in 1871, reflecting the dramatic increase in harbor activity. For a brief period, the Bridgeport Lighthouse was one of the nation's armed lights. During the Spanish-American War, a battery of 10-inch guns were installed to protect the harbor from Spanish warships. Just beyond the light is the ferryboat *Park City*, which operated between Bridgeport and Port Jefferson, Long Island. The lighthouse was demolished in 1953 after a fire.

BEER FOR PROSPERITY
WE WANT BEER

The signs alongside this truck on East Main Street read "Beer for Prosperity." The dry years during Prohibition caused many local residents heartache because of the loss of revenue. These fellows, however, seem to be taking it all in good spirit around 1932. From left to right are (first row) Tony Van, ? Pederson, John Corvino, Anthony Vena (in cab), and Paul Corvino; (second row) James Aurigemma, Bill LaBrenz, unidentified, Jim Sullivan, and Sal Supersano.

Inventor Buckminster Fuller used the old Locomobile factory at the foot of Main Street to build one of the strangest cars ever designed, the Dymaxion. Fuller and his partner, Starling Burgess, a yacht designer, built a sleek, three-wheeled vehicle that could run at a speed of 120 miles per hour. Although the Dymaxion was displayed at the 1933 World's Fair, the company went out of business by 1935.

DYMAXION - 7/28/33

KODAKS
CORBIT'S
CAMERA
SHOP
"WHERE CAMERA FANS MEET"
EVERYTHING
PHOTOGRAPHIC
COME IN AND GET ACQUAINTED!

Speaking of pride in work, many of the photographs used in this book were photographed by longtime Bridgeport photography studio Corbit's Camera Shop. Lewis Corbit Sr. and Lewis Corbit Jr. are responsible for documenting almost a century of Bridgeport history. Lewis Corbit Sr. opened his photography studio in 1907, the day of a disastrous fire on Steeplechase Island, and he never stopped taking photographs of the city's daily events. In fact, he was hired by the *New York Times* to cover events in Fairfield County. Lewis Corbit Jr. continued to run his father's business, a constant and familiar figure running around Bridgeport taking photographs. Thanks to Corbit Studios and to Edna Fransesconi, who preserved it for years to come. This photograph was taken by Corbit Studios in 1934. On the left is Lewis Corbit Jr., with his brother Lawson standing in the center.

The Southern New England Telephone Company formed in 1882, moving to several locations before settling in its art deco building of 1930 at John and Courtland Streets. Here Helen S. Cody takes a call in 1935.

The hurricane of 1938 caused considerable damage throughout the city, destroying many trees, particularly in Seaside Park and the surrounding South End. In this photograph, residents of Atlantic Street survey the uprooted tree in front of their houses. These houses were built in 1877 and designed by the Palliser Brothers, Bridgeport architects who sold their mail-order house plans throughout the United States.

Women work on the line inside the Frisbie factory in the late 1930s. Employees of the company would toss the pie tins around in the parking lot on their breaks. Kids would line up to buy pies after school, and they too would toss the tins. Many Bridgeport residents remember buying broken pies for only a nickel. In 1957, Wham-O Corporation changed the name to Frisbee when it designed the plastic disc fashioned after the original pie plate. The Frisbie bakery closed its doors in 1958. The pie tins are highly prized collectibles today.

FOUR

TOWARD THE MODERN ERA

The *Bridgeport Times-Star* lived a long and active life. First appearing as the *Farmer* in 1790, the newspaper continued under various names and finally emerged as the *Bridgeport Times-Star* in 1926. The offices of the *Times-Star* were in the old Seaside Club on Lafayette Boulevard. James L. McGovern (center, seated right) was the editor of the paper. The newspaper was known for its honest and nonpartisan reporting of local labor and immigrant issues. This photograph of the employees of the *Bridgeport Times-Star* was taken on the newspaper's final day of publication, November 25, 1941. A purchase of the paper for $200,000 by the owner of the competing *Bridgeport Post* surprised employees of the *Times-Star.* Given 30 minutes to vacate the premises, the *Bridgeport Post* sent a special crew to demolish the *Times-Star* presses.

TOPSTONE
CIGARS
ELODIE

BRIDGEPORT FLYER
DINER

Antonios J. Rountos emigrated from Greece, first living in New York City and finally settling in Bridgeport in 1941 because of a business opportunity. The West Side Bank gave Rountos an option to buy land on Fairfield Avenue, at the time an area covered with trees and pleasant greenery, reminiscent of his Greek homeland. An art deco, streamlined diner was brought in from Massachusetts and placed on the lot. Rountos opened the Bridgeport Flyer Diner and catered to the nearby factory workers and travelers on trips from New York to Boston–in the days before the expressway was built.

Platon Vlamis bought the hot dog business that was on the corner of Boston and Noble Avenues in 1949, keeping the old hot dog stand and the name Tomlinson for the business. Virtually just a shack with a grill inside and no seating, Tomlinson's had customers lining up outside the doors to have a chili dog or burger hot off the grill. The stand became a landmark where many a quick lunch was grabbed and by which directions were given. Many Bridgeporters could not pass by the corner without stopping for a "dog." The old stand was torn down in 2000, but a new, larger building with seating is currently on the same corner.

TOMLINSON'S
CHILI DOGS & CHEESEBURGERS
TOMLINSON'S
Hummel's
HOT DOGS
CHILI DOGS

GEORGE F. CARA

Here the crews of small wooden scows offload oysters onto the *George F. Carman*. The *Carman* is acting here as a "buy boat," purchasing juvenile, or seed oysters, off the scows. The oysters will be taken out to offshore beds next, where they will be grown to market size. When this c. 1950 photograph was taken, the captains of the scows received about 50¢ per bushel of oysters.

In 1941, the Bridgeport Bees started playing in Newfield Park. The professional minor-league squad played in the Colonial League. The Bees had several managers before Frank "Bud" Stapleton took on the job in 1950. Stapleton, who had previously managed other Bridgeport teams, stands next to his Chrysler with team members in Newfield Park on August 23, 1926.

TOPSTONE CIGAR FACTORY
TOP STONE
ELODIE
Cigars

Like nothing else, the smell of a good cigar can bring back memories. In Bridgeport, the Top Stone Cigar Company, at 256 Middle Street, provided cigars for generations of local residents. Top Stone Cigar was founded in 1903 by Edward Waegemans, a Belgian immigrant. The company used machines to roll some cigars, but special cigars like the Felipe Suave were rolled by hand. The Bridgeport business closed in the late 1970s. However, Top Stone cigars—now made in Florida—are still available at cigar stores.

Davidson's Fabric Store moved to its present location at 1242 Main Street in 1956. In 1989, Marshall Lewis's son Lance Lewis took over ownership of the store. Shown is Davidson's in 1956 on Main Street, just before the move. Note the signs in the window.

DAVIDSONS
Austins

HITCHING POST INN
Parking In Rear
FOR GUESTS
ONLY

During the War of 1812, Capt. Joel Thorp commanded the sloop *Othello*, which was captured by the British. This house on Lafayette Street is thought to have been built by Captain Thorp. Dating of the home varied between 1800 to 1835. Dr. Willard and Ella Fleck owned the house in later years. The house eventually became a restaurant known as Hitching Post Inn and was torn down in the 1960s.

Built to house the growing population of Bridgeport workers during World War I, this carefully planned development was one of the finest of several housing projects built in the city. The Bridgeport Housing Company developed planned neighborhoods like Seaside Village, with courtyards and small backyards, carefully laid out for families to own their own homes in privacy. This photograph was taken in 1963, showing the well-cared-for and shady streets.